Original title:
Twigs of Thought

Copyright © 2025 Creative Arts Management OÜ
All rights reserved.

Author: Jude Lancaster
ISBN HARDBACK: 978-1-80567-218-0
ISBN PAPERBACK: 978-1-80567-517-4

Leaves of Contemplation

Ideas flutter down like leaves,
Catching thoughts like squirrels weave.
A mental dance, we entertain,
Watch them spin, then fall like rain.

Chasing notions round the bend,
Like a joke you can't quite send.
Pondering where all the jest went,
Oh, the paths that thought could take!

Echoes in the Underbrush

Whispers bounce from tree to tree,
Like a strange, unfunny spree.
Muffled giggles on the ground,
As "What's that noise?" spins round and round.

Thoughts stumble, trip, and collide,
Like a clumsy critter that can't hide.
Echoes laughing through the leaves,
Who knew ideas could deceive?

Fractured Ideas

Snappy thoughts come in a blur,
Like a bee that starts to stir.
Then they fly, and oh so wide,
Buzz around, then back, they hide.

Jumbled up like socks in pairs,
Laughter springs from tangled snares.
Trying to recall the punchline,
But it's lost in thought's design!

The Forest of the Mind

Between the trunks, a riddle grows,
A snicker lurks where no one goes.
The branches wave in breezy glee,
A sorry pun stands proud and free.

Beneath the boughs, ideas crowd,
Some are shy, some bold and loud.
Yet in the shade, they tease and play,
In this wildwood, thoughts drift away.

Nature's Whispers

In the park, a squirrel danced,
Chasing acorns with a glance.
Birds gossip in a humorous tone,
While bees buzz 'bout their honeyed bone.

The trees chuckle in the breeze,
Tickling leaves, oh what a tease!
Mushrooms giggle, round and stout,
As the sun peeks in to pout.

Scribbles Among the Vines

In the garden, blooms converse,
Sharing secrets, oh how terse!
Roses boast of their bright attire,
While weeds plot pranks that never tire.

Grape vines tangle, tangled woes,
Whispering tales nobody knows.
Lettuce laughs when birds take flight,
Fancying greens with pure delight.

Spirals of Awareness

A snail ponders life's great race,
Taking time, a slow-paced grace.
A worm jests with the wiggle brigade,
In a soil party, plans are made.

Ants march in a curious line,
Mapping journeys, oh so fine!
Ladybugs paint their shells with pride,
While spiders weave a laugh inside.

Tangles of Reflection

In a puddle, a frog takes a leap,
Every splash brings laughter deep.
Foxes chatter with a sly intent,
As they plot their next mischief bent.

Clouds drift by, wearing silly hats,
While rabbits hop, avoiding spats.
In this woodland, whims abound,
Nature's jesters, pure joy found.

Secrets in the Sapling

In a tiny twig, secrets hide,
Like a squirrel with nowhere to slide.
It spills all the beans, oh what a fuss,
Whispering truths to the nearby bus.

"It's a tree-mendous day!" it shouts with glee,
While birds roll their eyes, can they just be free?
A leaf sneezes loudly, the sapling just cracks,
And laughter erupts from the old wooden tracks.

Solstice of Introspection

Under the sun, a ponderous tree,
Sipping on sap like it's fine green tea.
It stares at the clouds, giving them a wink,
As the bugs in its bark try hard not to blink.

"Oh, what should I do with this woodsy life?"
Said the tree with a laugh, avoiding all strife.
It embraced the odd thoughts, becoming quite bold,
While squirrels debated on braving the cold.

Rings of Contemplation

Counting my rings, what do they say?
Four were for laughter, one for the play.
A chipmunk chimes in, "Let's dance on the ground!"
Together they giggle, making quite a sound.

So deep in thought, or maybe just lost,
Each layer of memory comes with a cost.
But who can resist such whimsical charms?
When a tree tells stories, it surely disarms.

Serene Observations

High in the trees where the laughter flows,
A wise old branch nods as the chaos grows.
With each passing breeze, it giggles in glee,
Unraveling knots of the world's silly spree.

"Oh look," it remarks, "the sky is quite blue,
I think it's laughing at me, how 'bout you?"
The leaves all agree, with a whispering cheer,
As they sway in the joy of this whimsical sphere.

Draped in Silence

In the corner, secrets play,
Muffled giggles dance away.
A whisper's laugh, a shadow's pout,
Round and round, they twist about.

Underneath the cushion's care,
Lies a sock, a teddy bear.
Napping softly, they conspire,
Tickled fancies, never tire.

The cat's bemused, the dog's just snooze,
As chatter wraps in cozy blues.
Jokes exchanged in muffled tones,
Where every giggle feels at home.

Amid the silence, laughter blooms,
In the quiet, jesting fumes.
Socks and dreams in jumbled heaps,
In this silence, laughter leaps.

Threads of Solitude

In the corner, a single shoe,
Asks its partner, where are you?
With a chuckle, it stands alone,
A fashionista on its own!

A lonely pen begins to scribble,
Jokes in margins; it likes to giggle.
Each word a thread, spun with care,
Woven tales float in the air.

The clock laughs as it ticks away,
Mocking echoes of yesterday.
A solitary chair spins round,
In its whirl, lost thoughts are found.

Alone but not, the day drifts by,
Doodles bloom, as dreams fly high.
In this silence, fun ignites,
Witty whispers, silly sights.

Charms of the Thicket

In the thicket, where squirrels play,
I lost my hat on a sunny day.
A rabbit grinned, with quite a stare,
He wore my cap—what a fashion flair!

The bushes giggled, the trees did shake,
As I stumbled on, for goodness' sake.
A crow cawed loud, a real old tease,
Who said I should skip through the trees!

Underneath the Bark

Under the bark, ants held a show,
With tiny top hats, they'd steal the show.
A beetle so bold danced in a whirl,
While I laughed hard, my head in a twirl.

They offered me snacks, just crumbs of bread,
I thought 'No thanks!'—'tis purely their bread.
Yet under the bark, with a chuckle so deep,
I joined their fun—oh, the laughs we reap!

Ferns of Fancy

Whimsical ferns in a fanciful crowd,
Swirled in a jig, they laughed out loud.
One claimed it was just a warm-up dance,
While another twirled as if in a trance.

I watched them shimmy, those plants so spry,
With roots so wiggly, they could fly high!
In the midst of green, I found my cheer,
What a splendid stage! Bring me some beer!

Quietude Among the Leaves

In quietude, where whispers rise,
I found a frog in a clever disguise.
He croaked a tune, bold and brash,
I couldn't help but let out a laugh!

The leaves swung low and told a joke,
While I sat still, just a little stoked.
With giggles wrapped in the softest breeze,
Who knew the woods brought such delights with ease?

The Bark of Memory

A tree once lost its fancied hat,
Forgot it on a silly cat.
With every gust, it'd tease the ground,
Recalling moments, round and round.

The leaves chatter with tales so bold,
Of acorns lost and secrets told.
Barks laugh at knots, a twisted cheer,
Remembering youth without a fear.

Petals on the Breeze

Petals dance in a breezy swirl,
Giggling flowers in a dandelion whirl.
The bees hum tunes, like a buzz-band,
Making honey plans, all unplanned.

With every gust, giggles lurch,
As blossoms plot a playful search.
A sunflower jokes, 'I'm tall, you see!'
While grass snickers, 'You're just like me!'

Vines of Understanding

Twisting vines share tales absurd,
One bud said something quite unheard.
'Why do branches point this way?'
'It's just a game, don't disobey!'

The ivy grins, entwined in jest,
'Life's too short to take a rest.'
With laughter winding, they climb and crawl,
Making sense out of nonsense for all.

The Quiet Sapling

A little sprout with dreams so big,
Whispered jokes, a tiny gig.
'Why do trees wear hats of green?'
'It's just the style on the forest scene!'

In the shade, it plots its fun,
With roots that wiggle, just to run.
Ancient trees roll their eyes and say,
'Oh sapling, you'll grow up one day!'

Flourish of Whimsy

In a garden of giggles, the daisies dance,
Where bees wear sunglasses, taking a chance.
Thoughts swirl like petals in a playful breeze,
As thoughts on a trampoline bounce with great ease.

A mushroom in polka dots sings quite a tune,
Wishing for sunshine, and a trip to the moon.
Squirrels in tuxedos throw acorn confetti,
While clouds spill laughter, oh, isn't it petty?

Grasshoppers juggling, oh what a sight,
A ladybug winks, in the warm morning light.
Each flitting thought makes a humorous spark,
Like a firefly's laugh in the tickle of dark.

So join in this frolic, let your mind sway,
In a world full of nonsense, come laugh and play.
For the joy that we find in the silly and bright,
Turns branches of thought into pure delight.

The Canopy of Consideration

Underneath a canopy, thoughts twist and shout,
Where chipmunks debate who will dance in the bout.
A frog with a top hat reads philosophical books,
While butterflies giggle at the silliness in crooks.

Circles of wisdom spin tales so absurd,
As trees whisper secrets that can't be heard.
Each twig holds a letter, a note at the end,
Of a story where nonsense and giggles blend.

Curious thoughts lounge on a leafy old chair,
Sharing wise cracks with a raccoon with flair.
They ponder, they chuckle, in shadows they lay,
Inventing new games that turn serious gray.

Oh, the fun in the forest where laughter grows high,
With branches of wisdom that tickle the sky.
Revel in moments where thoughts frolic free,
For the joy of consideration roots deep like a tree.

Unraveled Branches

In a thicket of thinking, where ideas get spun,
A hedgehog named Stanley just can't stop the fun.
With pencils for quills, he sketches the night,
Drawing dreams that escape just before morning light.

As the foxes gather for their nightly debate,
They flip through old tomes, they giggle at fate.
"How can you be wise when you're only a fox?"
They share silly stories that tickle like socks.

Beneath tangled branches, a squirrel has decided,
To host the big party where nonsense is guided.
With nuts for the snacks and jokes on the menu,
Each laugh rings like bells, and joy feels like new.

Oh, the magic of thinking when tangled and wild,
Unraveled in humor, like a mischievous child.
Fluffy thoughts flutter, they leap and they dance,
Isn't life funny? Let's give it a chance!

Saplings of Serenity

In a patch of bright whimsy, saplings arise,
With thoughts like confetti that tickle the skies.
The daisies hold meetings, the bees write the laws,
Beneath boughs of laughter, where nature withdraws.

Silly ideas sprout like weeds in a lawn,
While bunnies do cha-chas right at the dawn.
Each giggle a raindrop, each chuckle a breeze,
Turn frowns into flowers with the greatest of ease.

A dandelion wishes to wear a top hat,
As a wiggly worm gives a wobbly pat.
They ponder the world while munching on cake,
Finding humor in mistakes that no one can fake.

So join this plantation of mirth and delight,
Where saplings and giggles grow taller each night.
In this garden of laughter where we all can gleam,
We shimmer and shine in the glow of a dream.

Blossoms of Wisdom

In the garden of chatter, I sit with my hat,
A sunflower gave me advice, just like that.
"Don't forget your roots, but dance a bit too,"
I laughed so hard, I spilled my green stew.

The daisies giggled, their heads bobbing low,
They whispered sweet secrets, putting on a show.
"Life's like the wind, it sways to and fro,"
I wondered if daisies also like to flow.

The roses chimed in, with petals so red,
"You can't take life too serious, it'll mess with your head!"
I agreed with a chuckle, then tripped on my shoe,
A tumble through blossoms, oh, what a view!

So here's to the garden, where laughter won't cease,
With flowers as sages, imparting their peace.
For wisdom is funny, and blooms in the sun,
In this whimsical patch, we all laugh as one.

Reveries in the Woodland

In a forest of dreams, with squirrels on the run,
A fox wore a tie, thought he'd just begun.
"I'm late for my meeting, oh, what a disgrace!"
I stifled my giggles, all over the place.

The owls exchanged jokes, deep in the trees,
"Why did the chicken fly? To follow the breeze!"
Their eyes were all wide, they hooted with cheer,
The forest was laughing, from far and near.

A rabbit in glasses read poems aloud,
"They say I'm too busy, but I'm really just proud!"
With a twitch of my nose, I joined in the fun,
In this woodland of laughter, each day's like a pun.

So let's romp through the pines, with giggles galore,
With critters and chuckles, who could ask for more?
In the heart of the green, with merriment grand,
The woodland's a haven, the funniest land.

Branches of Reflection

Up high in the trees, where the squirrels debate,
I found a wise owl who was wearing a plate.
"What's that on your head?" I couldn't hold back,
He smirked with delight, it was part of his act.

The branches swayed gently, with secrets to tell,
The laughter cascaded, like a musical bell.
A raccoon in a suit gave tips on great fortune,
"Just steal a few snacks, no need for a corporate!

With leaves all a-quiver, the sun peeked through,
"Life's an adventure; dress up, just like you!"
Said the wise old oak with his weathered bark grin,
So here in the treetops, we all spin to win.

Reflect on the fun, let the laughter flow wide,
With each funny tale that these branches provide.
In this canopy wonder, where chuckles ignite,
We find silly wisdom, and boy, is it bright!

Whispers in the Canopy

In the canopy high, where the whispers take flight,
A parrot confessed that he was quite bright.
"I've learned from the crows, who are cunning and sly,
They joke as they soar, always low in the sky."

With shadows that dance under leaves up so green,
The bugs shared their gossip, you won't believe what they seen!
"A snail told a turtle, 'I'm quick as can be,'"
The turtle just smiled, as slow as the sea.

The breeze brought a tickle, the branches did sway,
A chat with the wind, oh, what a bright day!
"Life's but a laugh, let's roll with the tide!"
The whispers kept coming, with giggles allied.

So listen quite closely, to nature's good cheer,
Where humor and joy drift in every sphere.
The canopy rumbles, with silliness bright,
In the heart of the green, everything feels right.

Woodland Reveries

In the woods, a squirrel danced,
Chasing shadows, it pranced.
A lost acorn rolled away,
Oh, what a funny display!

A beaver's hat, quite absurd,
Said, "I'm stylish, haven't you heard?"
But twigs kept falling from his head,
Fashion's tough in the stream bed!

The owl laughed at a sunburned fox,
Trying to climb, but got stuck in a box.
"Where's my sunscreen?" he quipped in haste,
Nature's humor, a lighthearted taste.

A pine tree's sneeze, quite the surprise,
Turned all the birds into flailing flies.
In the woodland, fun's what we're about,
Laughing 'til the sun's going out!

Entwined Realities

Two vines tangled in a breeze,
Claiming, "Life's a game, if you please!"
The flowers giggled as they spun,
Saying, "Let's dance and have some fun!"

The path seemed straight, but took a bend,
A lost raccoon called, "Can you lend?"
With cookies tucked beneath his paw,
His logic followed nature's law!

A rabbit sported mismatched socks,
Said, "Fashion's wild in woodland blocks!"
He strutted proudly, caressed by grass,
The critters cheered as he did pass.

Under flapping leaves, a toad croaked loud,
"In this merry place, I stand so proud!"
Nature chuckled in a playful glow,
Entwined, they danced in a vibrant show!

The Drift of Memories

In a glade, a pine tree spoke,
"Remember when I tried to poke?
A passing deer, so bold and spry,
It jumped so high, I thought it'd fly!"

A crow cawed tales of days gone by,
While chasing bugs that flew too high.
"I once lost a bet to a silly mule,
Now I wear a hat—ain't that a fool?"

The brook laughed softly, tickling rocks,
While frogs held court and read their stocks.
"Invest in flies; it's all the rage!"
Nature's comedy—turning the page.

With each chuckle, the leaves would sway,
As memories drifted, come what may.
The forest hums a joyful tune,
Where laughter echoes 'neath the moon!

The Solitude of Branches

In solitude, one branch did sigh,
"I dream of clouds that float nearby."
A bird perched high, asked with a grin,
"Are you waiting for the wind to spin?"

A leaf replied with playful flair,
"I'd dance all day without a care!"
But gusts of laughter tore it free,
Twirling round, as wild as can be.

An acorn tried to start a trend,
Declaring, "I'm a nut—just pretend!"
But rolling down with quite a splash,
It tumbled over in a flash!

Yet branches feel love in every sway,
Even solitude holds joy each day.
Nature's quirky tapestry we weave,
In laughter, we truly believe!

Flowing with the Current

A river flows, it twists and bends,
With rubber ducks, it makes amends.
A fish in a wig, it swims with glee,
While paddling ducks join in for tea.

The frogs wear hats, the crabs dance jigs,
As turtles race on tiny rigs.
The sun plays peek, from leaf to log,
And whispers secrets to a frog.

Trees gossip softly, swaying side to side,
While a breeze delivers the latest tide.
A squirrel sports shades, a chipmunk spins,
In the water's laughter, everyone wins.

So let's float on this merry stream,
Join the parade, and live the dream.
The current calls with a chuckle so bright,
In this splashy world, laugh with delight.

The Dance of the Dappled Light

In the garden, sunlight plays,
Like a kitten in a sunny maze.
Dancers flutter, twirl, and sway,
With butterflies joining the ballet.

A ladybug spins, in red and black,
While ants form a line, obeying the track.
The daisies cheer with giggles and claps,
As bumblebees take their boisterous laps.

The shadows leap, then come to rest,
In this oddball waltz, it's all a jest.
A snail in a tux, all shiny and bright,
Slides on in, with sheer delight.

And when the sun tips into yawning night,
The stars join in, all sparkly and bright.
So tiptoe along this whimsical floor,
In dappled light, let laughter soar.

Somnolent Branches

Branches yawn with sleepy glee,
As snoozing owls count one, two, three.
A raccoon's snore echoes through the night,
While a squirrel dreams of lofty heights.

The bees doze off in flowers' embrace,
With visions of honey in a sweet place.
The moon is a blanket, soft and round,
Wrapping the world in slumbering sound.

A restless breeze tickles the leaves,
As night critters hold conversations like thieves.
The stars play cards, with a wink and a nod,
While fireflies twinkle, a flickering squad.

So in this sleep, where silliness hums,
Dream on, dear friends, till morning comes.
When sunbeams break, all giggles will reign,
And nature awakens, a happy refrain.

Dreamcatcher of the Wild

In the forest, where giggles roam,
A dreamcatcher spins, creating a home.
Squirrels share dreams of acorn delight,
While rabbits hop to the playful height.

A fox winks at stars strung like beads,
Collecting laughter from grasses and seeds.
Mice in pajamas gather 'round,
Sharing tall tales of things they found.

Through rustling leaves, whispers fly,
Of a floating fish, and a butterfly.
The moon in the woods grins with glee,
As creatures dance wildly, wild and free.

So cast your dreams on this web so fine,
Where wonder and whimsy forever entwine.
With a clap of paws and a flick of the tail,
In this enchanting world, let joy prevail.

Sprouts of Imagination

In the garden of my brain, weeds grow tall,
Ideas pop like popcorn, one and all.
Dandelions whisper silly tunes,
While I chase thoughts like playful raccoons.

The tree of nonsense sways in the breeze,
With branches that tickle and tease.
Bouncing around like a rubber ball,
Each sprout is a giggle, a tiny sprawl.

Bright colors splatter like paint in a fight,
Imagination dances in pure delight.
Twirling and swirling through the air,
A carnival of dreams, with joy to share.

I skip through this vivid, chaotic space,
With a cartoon smile plastered on my face.
In this wild garden, I'll make my stand,
Where laughter grows, oh so unplanned!

The Subtle Rustle

Listen closely, my curious friend,
To the giggling leaves that twist and bend.
They gossip about the clouds above,
In their playful whispers, is a gentle shove.

A breeze carries jokes that tickle the sky,
As branches sway and birds fly by.
Their chatter brings smiles, a shared delight,
As shadows dance in the fading light.

One cheeky branch pokes another one low,
'Hey, don't be a stick, let's put on a show!'
The rustle grows louder, a mischievous tale,
Where every flutter is destined to sail.

Together they weave a fabric of fun,
With laughter as bright as the warming sun.
A subtle rustle, a symphony sweet,
In this forest of mirth, life's a playful treat!

Old Roots, New Dreams

Beneath the surface, where secrets lay,
Old roots chuckle at the light of day.
They sprout up stories, some dusty and bold,
And share their wisdom, a joy to behold.

New dreams bloom like flowers in spring,
With petals of laughter that twirl and swing.
Each thought, a seed sown in the soil,
Cracking up silently, ready to coil.

The old roots grumble, 'We've seen it all,'
As new dreams bounce, having a ball.
They make quite the pair, a jester's delight,
Old and new, dancing through the night.

So let's gather around, plant thoughts in a row,
Water them well, give 'em room to grow.
In this jolly patch, where silliness gleams,
We'll cherish both roots and our wildest dreams!

Foliage of Whimsy

In a forest of folly, where giggles reside,
Foliage of whimsy takes us for a ride.
Laughter unfurls like leaves in the air,
Sprinkling gladness everywhere!

Branches adorned with hats and shoes,
Swaying to rhythms of the silliest blues.
They throw a party with snacks galore,
While critters join in for the uproar.

With each rustling leaf, a new joke appears,
Tickling the funny bone, banishing fears.
The trees spark joy, like a tickling breeze,
As we gather 'round to share our glees.

In this quirky grove, let's dance and twirl,
With foliage of whimsy that makes our hearts whirl.
Embracing the laughter that nature does yield,
In this vibrant world, our joys are revealed!

Hushed Conversations

In the garden, secrets bloom,
Whispers hide beneath the gloom.
A squirrel listens, one eyebrow raised,
As flowers gossip, all amazed.

The daisies chuckle at the rose,
Saying, "How much perfume do you pose?"
The daisies tease, "You can't outshine,
We've got the sun, you can't so fine!"

Underneath the old oak tree,
A beetle's dance, a sight to see.
They chatter on, a gathering spree,
While ants march on, as busy as can be.

But then the breeze, it starts to hum,
The laughter softens, feelings numb.
In nature's midst, they laugh and sigh,
In hushed tones, where secrets lie.

The Weight of the Branches

The branches bend with tales to tell,
Of nutty acorns and weeds that fell.
"I'm tired," sighed a weary limb,
"Why's every bird a juggling whim?"

The chirping crew just flits about,
"Let's take a break, there's no doubt!"
A branch exclaimed, "I need a rest,
These tales are fun, but I'm too stressed!"

The wind replied with a cheeky grin,
"Hold your leaves, it's time to spin!"
With a whimsical swirl, the branches shook,
Releasing the tales like an open book.

And as the sun began to set,
They chuckled softly, no signs of regret.
For every weight that nature bears,
Is lightened with laughter, no room for cares.

Mindful in the Glade

In the glade where mushrooms sprout,
Fungi chat and sing out loud.
They ponder life, with silly glee,
"Should we start a band? What tune shall it be?"

A rabbit hops forth with a beat,
"Dance to my rhythm, let's move our feet!"
With clumsy paws, they jig and prance,
While flowers sway in an unplanned dance.

A toadstool pipes in with a joke,
"Why did the leaf bring a cloak?"
"Because it felt a bit too green,
And wanted to try a different scene!"

Together they laugh, a jolly crew,
Finding joy in the bizarre and new.
In the glade, under the sun's warm might,
Mindful moments make the day bright.

Perspectives Underfoot

The ants debate on who's the best,
While stepping stones just want to rest.
"Hey, we support you every day!
Without us, you'd just drift away!"

Gravel chuckles, "I'm the star,
You tiny folks don't go too far!
With every stomp upon my face,
You all get 'bumped' in quite a race!"

The daisies giggle from the rise,
As clouds whisper tricky lies.
"Do you hear what they are saying?
At our level, they're just playing!"

So down below, where odds collide,
The groundlings share a joyful ride.
In perspectives low, laughs are bright,
Where ants and stones find pure delight.

The Song of the Sidings

In the yard where thoughts collide,
A train of dreams takes its ride.
Each car filled with jester's glee,
Chugging along with silly esprit.

The cows wear hats, the ducks dance too,
A parade of fun in whimsical hue.
Whistles blow, laughter twirls,
As the engine of joy unfurls.

Tracks twist and swerve with delight,
While rabbits race in sheer light.
With every turn, a new jest grows,
As the freight of frolic overflows.

So hop aboard this comical train,
Leave behind your mundane strain.
With every sight, the laughter spreads,
In the song of sidelines, say what you said!

A Delicate Tangle

In a garden of thoughts, quite bizarre,
Butterflies wear glasses and go too far.
Tangled yarn and giggling weeds,
Whispering secrets of their silly deeds.

The flowers argue who wore the best,
While daisies play tag, they never rest.
A bee with a hat shares a funny tale,
Of how he once tried to ride a snail.

Vines twist like they're dancing, oh so grand,
Every leaf has a joke it planned.
The chirping birds sing a tune,
As the sun chuckles in the afternoon.

So join in the mess of merriment bright,
Where laughter finds the heart's delight.
In this tangle of joy, take a chance,
And sway with the flora in a merry dance!

Beyond the Trunk

Far beyond where shadows play,
Lies a realm where critters sway.
Squirrels strut in tailored suits,
While the earthworms tap in little boots.

A tree trunk boasts of tales so grand,
Of unicycles and a marching band.
Fungi giggle in cushioned tow,
As the ants line up for the talent show.

Beneath the boughs, a scene unfolds,
With whimsy wrapped in playful folds.
Every branch a platform for cheer,
As laughter resonates, oh so clear.

So venture forth, let spirits pluck,
Beyond the trunk, unlock the luck.
With every rustle, a chuckle is born,
In this enchanted place, we are never forlorn!

The Wisps of the Wilderness

Where the wild whispers with a grin,
A babbling brook leads you in.
Fireflies flicker in bow ties bright,
While owls hoot puns in the moonlight.

Each rustling leaf shares a joke or two,
As mischief lingers in the dew.
A hedgehog wears a crown of thorns,
And dances with pride as the night adorns.

The stars giggle in twinkling light,
As rabbits race in a comical flight.
Mushrooms gossip, exchanging a laugh,
In this wilderness, there's joy by the calf.

So roam the wild with spirits so free,
Embrace the whims of the bough and brie.
With every step, let joy take flight,
In the wisps of wilderness, pure delight!

Tendrils of Reflection

I pondered life while stuck in traffic,
The squirrel crossed, his moves so graphic.
I thought, 'What if he has a plan?'
Chasing dreams, or just a nutty man?

My coffee spills, a brownish lake,
A splash of wisdom, or a big mistake?
Perhaps it's fate, this morning mess,
Or just my need for a little less stress.

A cat on a fence, high as can be,
Staring down like he owns this tree.
"How I wish," I thought, "to leap and reduce,
The troubles of life to a single excuse!"

We dance through days like ants on a scene,
Chasing crumbs, so absurd, yet so keen.
What is clarity? A tweaked mindset?
Or just laughing at the small stuff we get!

Roots of Inquiry

Why do socks vanish in the wash?
Perhaps they're off to a sock-washing posh.
I ask and ask, but they just don't say,
Maybe they're on holiday- hey, what a day!

I questioned a tree: 'What's your secret?'
It rustled and sighed, told me to see the exit.
"In life's fun house, don't overthink,
Just swing 'round and grab another drink!"

Then there was a worm, so wiggly sly,
Telling me stories, oh my, oh my!
"Life's about digging, what more could there be?
Loosen your grip, let it all roam free!"

A ladybug laughed, thought I was daft,
"Come join my dance, take a break from the craft!
Roots may ask questions, but wings want to fly,
So let's be silly; just give it a try!

Swaying Structures of Mind

My thoughts are like branches, so frail yet bold,
In a gust of wind, their stories unfold.
I tried to catch one, it slipped right away,
'Hey, mind! Don't run off, come back here and play!'

I reasoned with logic, but it played peek-a-boo,
Hiding in riddles, just for my view.
"Oh come now, dear brain, don't be such a tease,
Let me connect dots while I swim in the breeze!"

A butterfly landed, winked with a grin,
"Your ideas are scattered; bring 'em back in!"
So I gathered my thoughts, as I swayed to the beat,
Twisting and turning, no shame in retreat.

With laughter in chaos, I found my delight,
In the tangled up dance of the day and the night.
Let's sway with the awkward, embrace every curve,
For in funny reflection, we all have the nerve!

A Dance of Ferns

In a shady glen, where ferns do sway,
I ponder the puzzles that playfully stray.
What if ferns giggle with each gentle breeze,
Blushing in shades of bright, leafy green tease?

A ladybug twirls what a sight to behold,
As I trip on my thoughts, a tad uncontrolled.
"Let's dance in the sun," said the shimmer of leaves,
"Join me, it's fun! Just breathe and believe!"

The breeze whispers secrets, a soft, silly tune,
Two squirrels pass by, they nibble on moon.
"Don't question too much, just leap and enjoy,
Life's a funny game, like a cheeky ploy!"

With laughter in steps, we round and we twist,
Wobbling light-heartedly, can't help but insist.
As ferns hold a party, we all join the spree,
For in nature's own jest, we all want to be!

Murmurs from the Soil

In the dark, the roots all chat,
About the rain, the sun, the cat.
Worms tell tales of juicy treats,
While ants are marching, tapping beats.

"Mud is fine," says one old leaf,
"As good as wine, or so I believe!"
The daisies giggle at the smell,
Of soil's rich tales, they know so well.

"Who dropped that beet?" a beetle quips,
"Must be the squirrel with acorn trips!"
Laughter grows beneath the ground,
As whispers swirl and spins around.

And when the rain begins to fall,
The gossip spreads, it's fun for all!
Roots and seeds beneath the haze,
Murmurs echo through their maze.

Ripples in the Understory

Under leaves, where shadows dance,
Frogs and critters take a chance.
"Did you see that jump?" they croak,
"It splashed so loud, I thought it spoke!"

The mushrooms giggle, "What a sight!
That jumpy fellow may take flight!"
A squirrel laughs with a nut in hand,
"Is that a frog's interpretive stand?"

Each ripple stirs the quiet ground,
As laughter echoes all around.
"Who's the king of the dirt?" they boast,
"It's me!" claims a gopher with a toast.

"Cheese and crumbs, for every fool,
Let's dance around the muddy pool!"
And with a splash, the fun ignites,
As nature joins the silly sights.

Scraps of Reflection

Piles of leaves, a cozy throne,
Where starlit dreams get gently sown.
Squirrels ponder in their lofty nest,
"Why do humans need to rest?"

Atop the hill, a raccoon grins,
"Let's throw a party, invite the bins!"
They gather scraps from every lane,
To share their finds and break the brain.

"Oh, the joys of trashy art,
Last week I found a rusty part!"
The moonlight beams like bright confetti,
As laughter flows, their minds are ready.

Reflections dance in the night air,
"What's next?" they ask in a grand affair.
From bits of junk, they find delight,
Scraps of fun in the starry light.

The Elder Tree Speaks

With bark so wise and branches high,
The elder tree lets out a sigh.
"Gather 'round, come hear my tale,
Of squirrels, seeds, and nutty trails."

"They say the grass is greener here,
But have you checked? It's full of cheer!"
The leaves all rustle, "What a jest!
Of every plant, I'm surely best!"

Fall winds whisper, tickling the boughs,
"You're only grand when still, dear cows!"
So roots and branches share a grin,
While woodland friends join in the din.

"Let's toast to laughter, loud and clear,
For every moment is a cheer!
Under this shade, we thrive in jest,
With tales of folly, we're truly blessed!"

Echoing in the Grove

In the grove where shadows dance,
Whispers giggle, take a chance.
Trees wear hats, quite out of style,
Squirrels debate, it's all worthwhile.

Chirping birds, they sing a tune,
Rabbits hop beneath the moon.
Leaves gossip, rustling tales,
Of wandering winds and epic fails.

The wise old owl nods in glee,
As crickets hold their symphony.
Nature's jesters, a merry band,
Crafting laughs, it's simply grand!

Echoes bounce, a joyful sound,
In this grove where fun is found.
With every step, the humor swells,
As nature rings its cheerful bells.

Stems of Perception

The stems around start to plot,
Reshaping thoughts, give them a shot.
Twirling whimsies, they confound,
Roots of laughter underground.

A backwards tree, it swings and sways,
Waves to flowers in funny ways.
Bees with goggles buzz on high,
Mapping trails that lead to pies.

A dandelion dons a crown,
Rusty signposts, upside-down.
They share opinions, wild and free,
On how to brew the best cup of tea.

With chuckles shared and quips exchanged,
The garden's antics are arranged.
Breathing in jokes with every breeze,
Nature's humor, sure to please!

The Forest of Ideas

In the forest, thoughts collide,
A merry band, they take a ride.
Pine cones laughing, rolling by,
As giggling grasses kiss the sky.

Branches stretch, they play charades,
Bark-faced trees on antics trade.
The weather vane spins and sways,
Plotting mischief for the days.

Puddles whisper, "Splash and cheer!"
While maples offer sweet ideas.
Snakes in ties debate the facts,
Inventing stories, full of acts.

With every leaf that flutters low,
New tales sprout amidst the glow.
In this forest, laughter reigns,
Where every root connects the brains.

Insights Beneath the Bark

Beneath the bark, secrets hide,
With giggles tethered, bold inside.
Raccoons conspire, plotting schemes,
Inventing wild, impossible dreams.

A whispering breeze, it cracks a joke,
As wisest trees begin to poke.
Squirrels scurry, tails held high,
"Muffins in the sky! Oh my!"

Branches twitch, they join the fun,
While ants compete, they race and run.
Beneath the sun, the woodland gleams,
Crafting smiles, beyond the dreams.

Each sundown brings a punchline grand,
As shadows stretch across the land.
In nature's heart, the laughs embark,
With every twist, insights spark!

Branches of Reflection

In the forest of my brain,
Ideas grow like little trees.
Some are tall, some are plain,
Others dance in the breeze.

One branch claims to be profound,
While others giggle, just for fun.
I wonder if they're tightly bound,
Or just twirling in the sun.

There's a root that's lost its way,
Spouting nonsense, full of cheer.
I laugh at what it has to say,
As I sip my cup of beer.

Each leaf whispers its own jest,
A punchline hidden from the norm.
In this jungle, I feel blessed,
Where silliness takes form.

Whispers in the Canopy

The chatter up above is bright,
As squirrels plot their silly schemes.
One forgot his acorn bite,
And now he's lost in wild dreams.

Birds gossip about the breeze,
Tweeting tales of absurd delight.
One swears he tripped on the trees,
As he tried to take flight.

A rustle here, a chuckle there,
Leaves giggle beneath the sun.
Nature's stage, a lively lair,
Where all the wild things run.

With each tickle from the wind,
I chuckle at the leafy sound.
In this canopy, I'm pinned,
To joy that knows no ground.

Fragments of the Mind

In corners where ideas roam,
Little sparks take shape and spin.
Some are bright, and some feel home,
While others just wear a grin.

A thought gets stuck, it starts a fight,
With logic that's gone for a stroll.
It trades a joke, then takes a flight,
Leaving reason with a hole.

Fragments flutter, dance around,
Some collide and burst with cheer.
Each mishap makes a silly sound,
While chaos shakes off fear.

In this wacky mental place,
Every whim needs to unwind.
I laugh and dance with lovely grace,
These are fragments of my mind.

Echoes of the Underbrush

In the underbrush, echoes play,
Rustling leaves with rampant glee.
Critters shout, "What's the game today?
Are we pondering or just carefree?"

A hedgehog spins a tall tale,
About a snail who wore a hat.
The chorus joins, "Let's set sail!
Find the mythic dancing cat!"

Laughter ripples through the ground,
As shadows prance beneath the trees.
With every whisper, joy is found,
It's a party on the breeze!

Echoes giggle, float, and twirl,
Magic lingers in nature's clutch.
Where bizarre thoughts begin to swirl,
And everything's a delightful touch.

Serpentine Musings

I pondered why the turtle crossed,
He sought the grass, but got lost.
A snail rushed past, with great delight,
Said, "Take your time, we'll be all right!"

The squirrel danced upon a branch,
In his top hat, did a little prance.
He juggled acorns, oh what flair,
The birds just stared, in utter stare!

Then came the frog, a sage, it seems,
With wisdom from his puddly dreams.
"Life is but a hop and skip," he said,
"Watch out for flies, and avoid the spread!"

So here I sit, with thoughts that twine,
A circus here, with humor fine.
Nature's jesters, in leafy toss,
In a world where logic is at a loss.

Fronds of Inquiry

When did the caterpillar think,
While munching leaves, at the brink?
"Should I be green? Or bright and bold?"
Such ponderings, never quite old.

The parrot squawked, cocked his head,
"Choose flair, my friend, don't live in dread!"
As crickets chirped a nightly song,
I wondered where the ants belong.

The wise old owl, with spectacles round,
Spoke of mysteries that abound.
"Who makes the rules? Is it the breeze?
Or the monkeys swinging from the trees?"

So up I climbed, to reach a peak,
A far-off thought, a little cheek.
In every branch, and every sway,
Jokes hide within the light of day.

Shadows Beneath the Boughs

Under branches, laughter strays,
As shadows dance in funny ways.
A rabbit sneezed, a startled jump,
Slipped on a leaf, and landed with a thump!

The hedgehog chuckled, rolled in mirth,
"Why did you bring that leaf to earth?"
While fireflies twinkled, lighting the ground,
A ballet of critters, so blissfully unbound.

The deer, confused, took a graceful leap,
Worried not of secrets to keep.
In their joyous romp, the night just sighed,
And beneath the boughs, I laughed and cried.

I scribbled notes that smiled so wide,
In this forest, there's nothing to hide.
With each rustle, a story birthed,
Funny fables from nature's girth.

The Quiet Grove

In the quiet grove, a cricket croaked,
His wisdom shared, or was it joked?
"Just keep it light, don't take the strain,
Unless, of course, you dance in the rain!"

An old, wise tortoise found his chat,
He spoke of cheese and how dogs sat.
"Life's like a picnic, don't forget the fun,
Chase after dreams, no need to run!"

Beneath the shade, the winds conspire,
With gusts that tickle, never tire.
A ladybug giggled, doing a twirl,
She declared, "I'm the dancing girl!"

So as I sat, my heart did bloom,
In a space where laughter filled the room.
Nature's whimsy, a carnival bright,
In the quiet grove, pure delight.

Flickers of Insight

In the forest of my brain, a squirrel darts,
Chasing shadows, playing tricks, where wisdom departs.
A chipmunk whispers secrets in a squeaky squeal,
While I ponder life's riddles with a banana peel.

Wisdom sometimes wears a hat that's too tight,
Making me giggle in the soft moonlight.
As branches sway with laughter, the breeze sings,
Of silly ideas hiding beneath feathered wings.

A wise old owl offers a clap of its wings,
But I'm busy counting all the funny little things.
The leaves rustle secrets, teasing like friends,
As I tumble on thoughts that dance and bend.

Each twig bends with humor, tales to unwind,
Cracking up at my thoughts, they'd surely be blind.
In this forest of jest, I find my light,
As wisdom and laughter join in the night.

Patterns Among the Roots

Roots tangled in laughter, they twist and they twine,
Like a jester's dance, always crossing the line.
Planted deep in the soil, they gossip and jest,
Turning serious matters into a comical quest.

Each knot tells a story, each curl brings a smile,
While worms wiggle around with absolute style.
They tickle the earth as they dig for their fate,
Proving that wisdom can come just too late.

The mushrooms join in, sporting hats of delight,
Winking at ferns, as they sway in the night.
A chorus of giggles, from trunks standing tall,
Echo in rhythms like a nature-born call.

In this quirky forest, we all do our part,
As laughter runs deep, like roots of the heart.
Patterns arise that make no sense at all,
Yet wisdom finds a way to have a good brawl.

The Breath of the Trees

Trees giggle and chuckle as they whisper and sway,
A cacophony of glee in the light of the day.
Their leaves wave like hands, inviting us near,
To share in the odd thoughts they hold dear.

With trunks that bark jokes, they wobble with glee,
Telling tales of squirrels who got stuck in a tree.
Their breath smells like pine mixed with jest and surprise,
As branches hold court under the wide-open skies.

Breezes carry laughter, rustling through the air,
Reminding me, perhaps, I shouldn't overprepare.
For wisdom insists there's fun to be found,
In the silly exchanges of life all around.

So I sit with my trees, in their shade and their cheer,
Learning life's lessons, one giggle at a time here.
In the breath of the woods, wise whispers unfold,
In the heart of the green, where humor is gold.

A Canopy of Dreams

Up above in the branches, where dreams like to float,
Are ideas that shimmer, like a whimsical boat.
The sun peeks through leaves, making shadows take flight,
As I watch my thoughts dance, oh what a delight!

A family of birds squawk with views quite absurd,
Debating on topics like who's the best bird.
While critters below hold a grand comedy night,
Cracking jokes 'bout the moon, under stars shining bright.

This canopy whispers, "Let's laugh till it hurts,
For wisdom's best served in the quirkiest shirts."
As jokes dangle down like fruit ready to fall,
I reach for the humor, embracing it all.

In this realm so enchanted, where ideas take wing,
I'm reminded that laughter is the finest of things.
For under this shelter of dreams woven tight,
I find joy in the laughter and giggles take flight.

Musings on the Breeze

A leaf in the wind takes a spin,
With playful antics, a giggle within.
It twirls and it sways, much like a dance,
Who knew trees had such a wild chance?

The acorns are laughing, quite full of glee,
As squirrels argue over the best spot for tea.
The branches all chuckle, their bark is so wise,
They tell jokes about clouds wearing silly ties.

Grass blades gossip about the sun's prank,
As shadows chase friends, they're off to the bank.
The flowers, they snicker at bees buzzing low,
Pretending the nectar's a secret they know.

So let's lift our spirits and sway to the tune,
Of nature's own laughter beneath the bright moon.
Here laughter is light, and joy hangs around,
In this whimsical forest, let bliss abound.

Filaments of Truth

A spider spins webs, a pure tangled mess,
Each strand whispers secrets of nature's finesse.
The bugs caught inside, with protest they shout,
"I thought I was meal, not a grand twist of clout!"

The flowers gossip, with petals so bold,
"Have you heard the grasshopper's tale that was told?
He leaped through the dew, all covered in green,
And mistook his own shadow for a new cuisine!"

The wise old oak chuckles at squirrels' blight,
"You hoard all the acorns, then lose them at night!"
With branches a-shake, he offers his thoughts,
"Life's jokes are the treasure, far more than your nuts!"

So ponder the quirks, as the sun starts to set,
Nature's giggles echo, so don't lose your bet.
When we share the laughter and dance through the trees,
Perhaps we'll discover the world's mysteries.

Nature's Dialogues

The critters convene, a wild little crowd,
In meetings of mischief, both squeaky and loud.
The rabbit speaks first, with a twitch of his ear,
"I heard from the hedgehog that springtime is near!"

The turtles all nod, with wisdom of ages,
"We've seen many springs in our slow-paced stages.
But consider the hares, they're plotting a race,
With bets on the line, it might quicken the pace!"

The birds start to chirp, their tunes intertwined,
"Hey, did you see that kid? Isn't he blind?
He ran through the bushes, all tangled in weeds,
And thought he was flying while tripping on seeds!"

Oh, how they all cackle, under the tall trees,
Where stories of folly hang light on the breeze.
Their talks are a treasure, a riot of cheer,
In this circle of nature, all laughter is dear.

The Gnarled Path

Winding and twisting, the trail has a grin,
Where rocks whisper secrets, and laughter begins.
The branches above laugh with leaves in full sway,
As travelers wonder which way they should stray.

A signpost is wobbling, with arrows askew,
"Left to the laughter, or right for the dew?"
The footpath giggles, a merry old chap,
"Follow me, friends, for a splashy mishap!"

Mushrooms poke out, with spots like a clown,
Saying, "Step on us once, we'll claim you a crown!"
While squirrels drop acorns, like candy from trees,
Watch where you're stepping, they might just tease!

Yet onwards they wander, through trees all askew,
Where bushes are gossiping, and skies are so blue.
Embrace the odd journey, enjoy every jest,
For laughter's the compass; it's truly the best.

A Meadow of Ideas

In fields of dreams, the cows wear hats,
Ideas sprout like mushrooms and chats.
Silly things dance under the sun,
While thoughts on roller skates have fun.

Bumblebees buzz with laughter so bright,
Tickling daisies that sway left and right.
The grass whispers jokes to the clouds above,
A meadow of giggles wrapped in love.

Birds play chess on a fence post near,
While a squirrel juggles acorns with cheer.
Each blade of grass a story to tell,
In this quirky place, all is well.

Unicorns skip with a wink and a grin,
Chasing butterflies—oh, what a spin!
In this funny land where thoughts take flight,
Laughter and joy are the purest delight.

Lattice of Perception

Through frames of fancy, we weave our spree,
Thoughts play hide and seek, just like a bee.
Cats wear spectacles, dogs read the news,
While thoughts trade funny hats in a cruise.

Peeping out from behind the fence posts,
Giggling ideas, like playful ghosts.
Here, perspective is a curly fry,
Dancing on screens as we watch the sky.

Fish in bow ties discuss the weather,
Scribbling rainbows in a big old tether.
The lattice shakes with puzzling delight,
As thoughts jump around in sheer moonlight.

So catch a thought, give it a spin,
Let your imagination swirl and grin.
In this world of twists and spectacles,
All is more fun, whimsical miracles!

Timid Thoughts

Timid thoughts peek from under the bed,
Wearing pajamas, a blanket on head.
Whispering secrets to the dust bunnies,
Hiding in corners, where nothing's funny.

They tiptoe around, cautious and shy,
While giggling shadows pass swiftly by.
"Can we play too?" one timid thought squeaks,
As the laughter outside overflows and peaks.

A tickle of wind makes them quiver and sway,
As dreams in a jigsaw jump into play.
With pastels of humor they paint the air,
A timid thought's giggle, a soft, gentle flare.

So gather your worries and let them roam,
Invite each thought to find its home.
In this funny realm of nerves and glee,
The timid transform, wild, spirited, free!

Tendrils of the Imagination

Curly tendrils reach for the sky,
With humorous plants that giggle and sigh.
A banana peels jokes, a tree shares rhymes,
In the garden of nonsense, we bloom with chimes.

Worms with megaphones declare the news,
While daisies in boots strut out in their shoes.
Ideas twist like vines in a swirl,
Spinning tales from a whimsical whirl.

A cactus grows arms, giving hugs to the sun,
As all of creation shares jokes just for fun.
Imagination sprouts from the ground,
In this merry dance, joy knows no bound.

So nurture your thoughts, let them climb high,
In the trellis of laughter where birds fly by.
Let playful whispers tickle your soul,
In this garden of giggles, we become whole.

Reverie Among the Roots

In the garden, I did ponder,
Thinking thoughts that made me wander.
Should I grow a plant with luck?
Or maybe one that quacks and clucks?

A carrot wearing sunglasses bright,
Teasing rabbits with delight.
Would a tomato sing a song?
Or just sit there and tag along?

Shadows of Clarity

In the corner, shadows prance,
Giving the moon a silly glance.
They twirl with glee, a dance of light,
Until the cat says, "What a sight!"

A pickle's tossed across the floor,
It rolls and bounces, wants some more.
The fridge, it giggles at the show,
As sausages join in, all aglow.

An Oak of Understanding

Beneath the oak, I sit and chat,
With squirrels wearing tiny hats.
"Life's a nut!" one squirrel did say,
As they cracked jokes in a cheeky way.

An acorn fell and hit my head,
"Now you're wiser!" another said.
What wisdom can these critters share?
I ponder while I comb my hair.

The Horizon of the Heart

I painted clouds with shades of green,
In a world where nothing's as it seems.
Horizon giggled, 'Try to fly!'
But I just tripped and caught a sigh.

My heart took off, a daring flight,
Only to land in a dandelion's light.
"Next time, let's stick to the ground,"
I whispered as the floaters swirled around.

www.ingramcontent.com/pod-product-compliance
Lightning Source LLC
Chambersburg PA
CBHW071838160426
43209CB00003B/339